A Fly on the Wall

Mini Menon

BookLeaf Publishing
India | USA | UK

Made with ❤ on the BookLeaf Publishing Platform
www.bookleafpub.in
www.bookleafpub.com

To the people who have been instrumental in bringing change to my life.

My loving husband - Rajeev, daughter - Sanjana, parents - Leela and Mukundan Menon, sister- Nimi

and To Cinash

To all my irreplaceable, champion Friends

To everyone who has touched my life

To the regular person who has great potential to be the change

Acknowledgement

Books have interested me since childhood. Poems have always been an integral part of me growing up. I always enjoyed prose and poetry in school. My poems are my experiences of life. I love nature and that's where I draw my inspiration from. Daily life happenings are something I think deeply about. I believe life is complex and layered. Every coin has two sides to it. Every issue I encounter, I try and weigh the pros and cons. Also, I have my own takes on matters that impact this world. I always hope for a better, safer, and inclusive world.

My husband, Rajeev, has been my sounding board with a voice of his own. I am extremely grateful to him for bearing with all my poem ideations and travelling with me to the finished and unfinished poems. For letting me be in the times I was mulling over ideas.

My daughter, Sanjana, who brings great joy to my life. Her questioning and point of view is my growth.

My friend, Padma, for always encouraging me and believing in me. Our long discussions have helped me gain clarity on many a thoughts and feelings.

Thank you!

Preface

I have mostly been an observer throughout my life.

People, their behaviours, feelings have always caught my attention. The poems in this book are drawn from these observations and analyses of them.

I hope some of the poems resonate with you and some others help you grow and yet others you question and debate.

The remaining, you could let them rest in peace.

Poem-1

Naked she walked

Some laughed

Others scorned

What's wrong?

This is me

This is how I am created

So, what's the fuss about?

A mother walked up

To cover her up

Even though,

It was hard to breathe

Under all the wraps,

All eyes were off her

Relief it was!

Normalcy found friends

And soon fashion dictated

Few layers came off

Letting her breathe

She learnt to juggle

Between naked and completely covered

To everything in between

At times, she put others at unrest

And at other times she lived with the unrest

But the big revelation was

No matter whether naked or covered

She exists

And her name is TRUTH!!!

Poem-2

The birth of a baby is exhilarating

Yes, exhilarating and very joyous

For the parents, relatives

And even to strangers

Seeing a baby starts the ranting

"She looks like her mother"

"She has bright eyes"

"She has less hair"

And on and on

As many people

So many observations and advises

This little girl was born with a birth mark

Yes, with a black birthmark on her cheeks

Now, the observations got limited

To the birth mark

For the Just Born

Subconscious, unconscious learning

Was about the birth mark

“It is a sign of luck”

“She’s a girl, this could tarnish her beauty”

“It would be tough for her to be married”

"She could use a concealer"

As she grew so did the mark

Yes, the mark on her cheek

Seem to grow too

She was called

Map of Africa

Ms. Gorbachev

Ms. Spittoon

She cried her lungs out

Why am I different?

Why was I made different?

So out came the concealer

An extra effort every morning

One day heavy rains

Yes the heavy rains lashed out

The kind that washed away the top soil

Did the same to her face

A young boy standing across the road

Stared at her

Stared at her so hard

She hated the rain

All she wanted at this point

Was for the earth to part

And eat her up.

She ran home

Yes, she ran home as fast as her legs could

She looked in the mirror so hard

And the question that popped out was

Who am I?

The answers that began spilling

Were far too many

Oh really ???!!!

And without her realizing, the twitch on her lips

Broke into a smile

And her hands threw the concealer into the trash

Life suddenly changed

Yes, life changed for the better

It became easy and joyful

So now when somebody asked her

About the mark

She said

"Map of Africa"

"Ms. Gorbachev"

"Ms. Spittoon"

"And laughed along with them"

The focus on her far too many

Helped her become the best baker in town

Everyone, today, is talking of her pastries!!!

Poem-3

The bouquet of lilies

That came in the arms

Placed gently in the vase

Was slowly withering

Whether in its own home

Or somebody else's home

Wither it must

What makes it worthwhile

Is the amount of joy and fragrance

It brought to its own

And others' lives!

Poem-4

A little girl

From remote India

With two elder sisters

And a younger brother

Went to school

Where vernacular language

Was what she listened, spoke, read and wrote

The sound of the language

Was as pure as the river

That flowed there

As pure as the air

That blew there

As pure as the food

That was rustic and traditional

As pure as her smile

That radiated from her heart

The parents stuck

In traditional farming practices

Attributed natural calamities

To God's fury

When empty stomachs

Didn't let them sleep

When tattered clothes

Didn't cover them

When the future of the children

Didn't seem bright at all

The manmade progress in the city

Beckoned them

The confidence of educated in the city

Pulled them

The weather-independent jobs

Lured them

The little girl and her brother

Were the chosen ones to move along

Being cut off from school

Did not deter her spirits

Finding unorganized places

To help take her literacy forward

Embracing a foreign language

With the same purity as vernacular

When asked if she missed going to school

Pat came the reply

Who will look after my brother?

How will my parents go to work?

Poem-5

A lifeless body lay

People walking in, out and around

Does the body know their presence?

If the body could think what would it?

Would it know true from fake?

Would it care for all the respect?

Would it like to partake in the discussions?

What are the true feelings on the tears shed?

I was connected to your soul

We promised to share laughter

Our world was the whole world

While we were together

Today I met another part of your world

Whom I know from your eyes

They were very familiar

And yet very unfamiliar

Thank you dear friend

For letting me into your world

It's Hasta mañana

Till we meet again.

Poem-6

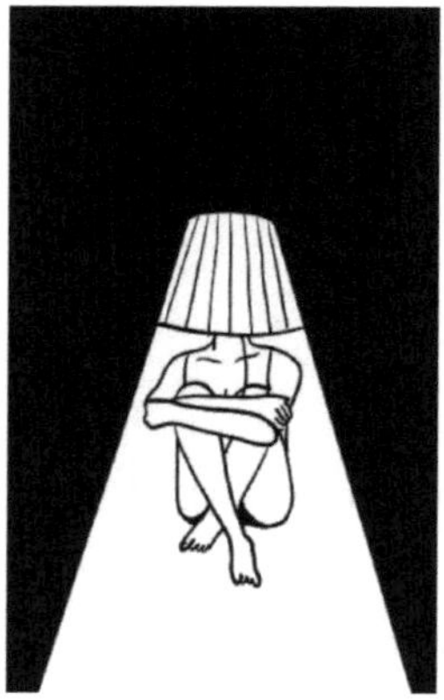

Sitting on the sofa

Stomach full

Staring at the television

Moving the glance

To the artwork on the wall

On to the other side

That overlooks a garden

And then asking the question

Is my life worthwhile?

Problem is true!

Problem cannot be denied

No problem is big or small

Problem is a problem. Period.

Problem has multiple solutions.

Feeling worthless is true!

Worthless cannot be denied

Worthless cannot be big or small.

Worthless is worthless. Period.

Worthless has multiple solutions.

Get up. Get moving.

Look around.

Focus on task at hand.

Find a task.

Be a helper.

No man is so poor to not give.

Find a taker.

Be a giver.

Enjoy the sunrise and sunset equally.

Poem-7

Many a dream accomplished

Many more ahead

Waiting to be achieved

Life is beckoning you

But death chooses you.

Pain is killing

Many more seem ahead

The downside is both

Physical and mental

Death is beckoning

But life chooses you.

We don't choose life and death

Life and death choose us!

Poem-8

The minute I make my entry

Shaking his whole body

He runs towards me

And is all over me.

Such expression of love

Who can resist?

When he is sick and can't move
My voice is a strength

To pick himself up

And come to me.

Such expression of love

Who can resist?

The food I make

World would judge

But not him

He licks it to the last morsel

Such expression of love

Who can resist?

I call him whatever I fancy

He still gazes at me lovingly

Still rotates around me

Like I am the sun.

Such expression of love

Who can resist?

When you want love

Be a canine friend.

Poem-9

Success is what I am seeking

Hard work is what I have put in

But I failed

After crying

Repeat

This time I pass

After sulking

Repeat

This time close to being the topper

After infuriating

Repeat

But status quo

Why can't I be the best?

What is the X-factor

God was the answer

Along with hard work I began pleading with God

But was not the topper

Repeat

Along with hard work I began bribing God

But was not the topper

Repeat

But status quo

How can I do different?

Shifting the focus around me

The realizations that dawned

The view for the topmost to top is same

The learnings are different

Soon obsession for topmost reduced

The peace that accompanied was priceless

Success is what I got!

Poem-10

The men who don't raise their voice

Against

The wrongdoings of their brothers

Are wrong.

The women who don't stand up

For

The sisters who have been wronged

Are wrong.

The politicians who don't join hands

With

The oppositions when they see wrong

Are wrong.

Women are safe who hide

Behind

Their brothers, fathers, husbands, sons but

Are wrong.

Anyone who thinks this planet does not belong

To

Man, woman, girl, boy, animals, insects, trees

Are wrong.

Someone who doesn't know how

To

Respect boundaries and be kind

Are wrong.

Everyone who preaches

protection, outfits, conversations, places to go

as against being

sensitive, evolving, listening, earth citizen

are wrong.

Nothing is permanent

Remember

The mighty will fall.

Poem-11

Have you seen

The snail with the spiral shell pattern

The grasshopper green, brown, yellow

The egg, caterpillar, moth before seeing the butterflies

The leaf miner who is like a toddler given a paper

The millipede's legs arranged differently from centipede

The itchy worm that reminds you of certain eyebrows

The slug that's so gluey

The earthworm with its transparent body

The leafcutter who makes best kirigami

The green lacewing who wins hide-and-seek

The pod borer who must be the teacher of cork borer

The dragonfly with the iridescent colors

The beetle with its true beauty

????????????????

If not think twice

You are missing

The major part of ecology

The reason for food on the table

The most diverse group of animals

The absence of which ceases human life

For

Little things do matter!

Poem-12

The teacher in the class

Pushing the topper

In the hope that

He brings laurels to the school

The teacher in the class

Working with the child

Who is lagging behind

In the hope that

He does not fail

The teacher in the class

Let me be

Who is right in the middle

In the hope that

I will pull myself through anyway

Sitting right in the middle

Me and the others like me

Notice

ONLY WE NOTICE

The Fly on the wall!

Poem-13

Teacher in the school

Teacher in the school

Lesson plans to be made

Activities to be designed

Material to be kept ready

Correction of children's books

Preparation for annual day

Absent colleagues class to be taken

Self-appraisal to be done

Oh! It is time for class

Oh! It is time for class

The innocent yet mischievous faces

Of 18 children staring at you

The smiles on their faces

Are so infectious

Without your knowledge

You begin to smile

The only prayer I have

The only prayer I have

Please let me make them

Love themselves

Respect themselves

Know their worth

Accept the weakness

Have no fear to speak their mind

Let them go home feeling

Let them go home feeling

I am good

I am nice

I am great!

Poem-14

Fashion is

The reflection in the mirror.

Should please my eyes

The colors, the fitting.

Fashion is

The comfort I feel.

Should please my body

When I sit, stand, walk, run, bend.

Fashion is

Sometimes a tiny bit

The look in others' eyes

Which make me blush, cringe

Fashion is

Sometimes a statement

To the society

That I matter.

Fashion is

Also an answer

To many a people

Who are quick to judge.

Poem-15

Waking up and the first thought

Hope my child slept well

Hope my mother's cough is better

Hope my dad makes it to the bank

Hope my husband's meeting goes well

Hope my friend is emotionally better

Hope I can complete tasks for the day

Do the laundry

Dust the house

Cook the dinner

Buy the books for my child

Pay the electricity bill

Prepare a topic to teach my child

Water the plants

Attend to the leaking tap

And they call me

“Not a working woman”.

Poem-16

Gratitude has the widest range

From just being able to breathe

To getting a million-dollar home.

From just being able to go to school

To getting admission in the best school.

From just being able to wear clothes

To be able to wear couture.

From just being able to eat food

To be able to have haute cuisine.

The truth of the matter is

Everybody has

Something to be grateful for

And something to cry about

What do you choose?

Poem-17

Dear Darkness,

How are you?

I am sure you are doing good.

The murders, the thefts, the abuse

Are all on the rise

All happens in your presence

Everyone hates you

The child, the girl, the woman, the old

And rightly so

After all, you remain a mute spectator.

Are you really party to all this?

What is your gain?

Are you just a sadist?

Is it your way of being in the news?

Or are you just an innocent victim?

Are you just as disturbed as many of us?

Do the characterless just use you as a cover?

Do you accept the blame as a parent would?

I am so confused now.

I hope you reply to me soon.

Until then

Bye from me.

Poem-18

Working hard to be comfortable

Wearing clothes, shoes that speaks comfort

Driving a vehicle that spells comfort

Making a home that screams comfort

And the constant improving upon comfort.

There is a flipside to comfort

The tattered and battered speaks

And are met with indifference of comfort

The broken civic amenities spells out loud

Are hit by the window of comfort

Natural calamities scream for help

Gets blocked by the walls of comfort

Poem-19

I am envious of my husband

When guests come home

He can sleep in peace through the night

While I remain awake in the dark

Planning and re-planning the next day

When he wakes up in the morning

The guest women are around him

Offering to make tea for him

Giving him a break from his daily tasks

As he takes a final sip of his tea

They grab the mug and into the sink

Wash, wash, utensils wash, wash

There goes his only job in the kitchen!

Why am I so oblivious to all these women guests?

I have been cooking for them

I have been making their beds

I have ensured their toiletries are in place

Finally they notice me

They gave me tips on

How I could enhance the dish I made

A better place to get a quilt

The list of vegan toiletries available

That just made me wish I remained in oblivion

I am envious of my husband

When we go as guests

He accepts all the pampering

With the best of his smiles

On the other hand I am lost

I sit like a queen for a while

Then get up and prowl around

I spot onions waiting to be chopped

I pick them and chef I become

The host gets guilty

Seeing her guilty I become guilty

We apologize for our guilty

And we split for a while

But my mind is working.

If you think I am complaining

No I am not

I am privileged

The value of being at home

All alone is not lonely at all

I am at peace

My independent husband is busy

How does he shift so easily from

Being independent to being dependent?

Is it conditioning by the society?

I don't know. All I know is

I am envious of my husband!

Poem-20

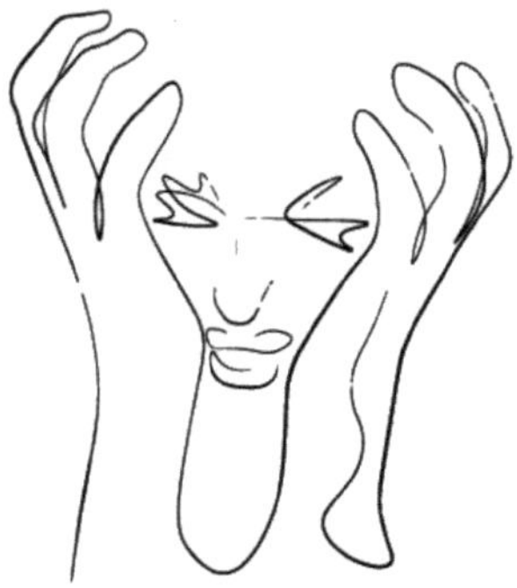

We were sitting in the same frame

I cooked for you

Was met with

The food is lacking

I am sorry

You missed my love and effort

I bought this gift for you

Was met with

This gift is lacking

I am sorry

You missed my love and effort

I put you up there

But you saw that as lacking

Thank you for teaching me

To respect my love and effort

Now you are calling me arrogant

You see more of my lacking

We are not sitting in the same frame.

Poem-21

I am a home citizen

I am a locality citizen

I am a city citizen

I am a state citizen

I am a country citizen

I am a global citizen

I am an Earth citizen

The growth has been gradual

But the most essential growth.

We should all hopefully

Become Earth citizens one day

Every life matters

Every abiotic matters

The balance is what makes the earth work

Let's think before creating and using anything

It is our responsibility towards the earth!

Poem-22

As a sapling

Every small shoot that showed up

Was celebrated

The growing branches

Unconsciously, very unconsciously

Began tangling with each other

The joys and pains of being together!

They tangled not to be untangled

Soon it was hard to distinguish

One from the other

And inseparable they became

Life without each other was unimaginable!

Unimaginable is achievable!

As a tree

Shed leaves gave way for new

The entangled branches

Sub-consciously, very sub-consciously

wanted to break free

A lesson learnt!

Tangling is easy

Disentangling is complicated

The pains and joys of breaking free!

The physical and emotional altercation

Is hard to explain

Life with each other is accepting change!

Change is the only constant!

As a full grown tree

Separating branches

Consciously, very consciously

Want to let go

That's when Spirituality kicks in!

The learning of which

Makes one - The Mother Earth

Encompassing everyone by

Attaching yet detaching

The big realization!

To start free

And end free!

Poem-23

The sound of the wind's music

The feel of raindrops

Falling on the head

The intoxicating fragrance of lotus and roses

The peacock dancing.

The dark cloud as the canvas

Makes a perfect time for the sun to paint

The rainbow.

And that makes a Magical day!!!

If you think it is too bookish

I can assure you

It happens!!

Take time off

To speed off

To places in remote India

Where luxury ends

And magic begins!!

Poem-24

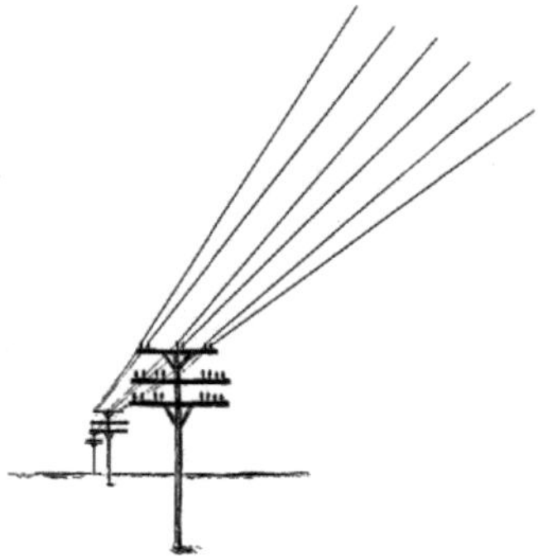

Two young migrant boys

On the expressway

Riding an old Luna

After paying toll charges

Perhaps, equal to the cost of the Luna!

The two boys

Cued in to the nuances of nature

The sun, rain, clouds, wind

Amidst the speeding cars!

The two boys

Had smiles on their faces

It was almost like the rainbows

Had descended on their lips!

Poem-25

The strong and the weak

Can be deceptive

It takes great experience to

Distinguish them

Be blessed if you or

Someone

In your life

Can recognise that

Poem-26

A big thorn tree

As big as an old mango tree

Stood at our fence

A tree with tiny leaves, big pointed needles

Unproductive to the common man

But not to my mother

Who got a branch cut

To bring out her creative side

Decorating to resemble a mini Christmas tree.

Little did we know

There was someone else

Waiting to bring out a creative side

One Summer, little yellow birds

In the size of sparrows

Became a regular visitor to the tree

Under our blind eyes

But not missing my mother's

Who was quick to show us

A nest in the making

Watching the home in progress

Was the first joy of home building

Within a fortnight

Hanging precariously

from an upper branch

Away from the trunk

Was a nest

And what a nest!

Made out of dry grass and twigs

A finish so impeccable

A thin esophagus closer to the branch

Extending downward to the stomach

Leading to a cut-short large intestine

Mankind is trained to look top-down

But this nest is bottom-up

With the entrance from below!

Soon three more similar homes appeared

Finding the name of this bird was a task

Finally the local gardener identified

It as Baya

So, Baya it was!

The Bayas constantly jabbered

Filling the air with warmth

Within the next fortnight

Little Bayas were born

The chitter-chatter grew by leaps

Just as winter was setting in

The Bayas just disappeared

The nests stood the test of time

Beating the heat, rain, wind, cold

We waited for next summer

But the Bayas didn't come to our tree

Later we spotted them

On a tree in a friend's garden.

From then on began our wait

Every summer

Which tree would the Bayas choose?

As for the nests on our tree

It was brought down

By the Gardner

Who endured bruises

Inflicted by the thorns

And this adorned my home

For the longest time

Much later we got to know

From the biology teacher

The Baya is also called

Weaver bird!

Poem-27

Stand up

Bow down

Be you

Be yourself!

Listen in

Understand out

Thoughts first adsorb

Then release or absorb

Build oneself

Be yourself

Be you!

Poem-28

O' Pigeon

The sounds of claps are nerve-wracking

The nets are up in the balconies

The spikes for birds are on Amazon

The adaptation skills are commendable

From a 20 to a 2 square feet place

The unwanted feeling is growing

Why are you still here?

How are you still here?

O' Pigeon

I see you everyday

Sitting here, flying there

Eating here, talking there

Pooping here, there, everywhere

What is the purpose of your life?

How do you live?

O' Human

Is love the only reason to live?

I respect the creator

The love with which I am made

The love that I even found in one human

Keeps me here

Looking after me and not hurting another

Is the sole purpose of my life

Pray tell me if you have any other purpose!

Poem-29

I talked to the papaya tree

How are you so tall and your fruits so delicious

The tree told me its story

Lonely was I, when thrown as a tiny little seed

Till I made friends with *Acceptance*

And I mingled with mud and water

The darkness inside the earth scared me

Till I made friends with *Brave*

And soon the dark little world looked bright

I was inside this monotonous world

Till I made friends with *Adaptable*

And feeding from the soil I grew bigger

I was hurt with people plucking and wind hitting

Till I made friends with *Resilience*

And I bounced back

I was feeling worthless

Till I made friends with *Thankful*

And I gave old leaves to the soil

I had no work to do

Till I made friends with *Teamwork*

And working with sunlight and soil-made food

Working seemed meaningless

Till I made friends with *Capabilities*

And flowers bloomed

I was restless about knowing me more

Till I made friends with *Patience*

And flowers turned into fruits

I was heavy with fruits

Till I made friends with *Giving*

And the squirrel, birds and children sang

I talked to the papaya tree......

Poem-30

It was an unusual bond

which had no legal stand.

Between a foursome

which was awesome.

A bond that was enviable

which was strongly unbelievable.

An old man and his wife

a mother and her little life.

The old man, a Santaclaus

Gifts came without a clause.

The old woman, a mother

Love came without a bother.

The mom a helper

ran errands without a flicker.

The little life entertained

kept smiles maintained.

There were no moments of unease

where laughter flowed with such ease.

Born to be together

never to face rough weather.

The old woman had an ailment

ceasing every single moment.

The old man fell ill

bringing laughter to a standstill.

Sickness of the two brought in kin

To take care of their well-bein'

The other two faded to avoid ambiguity

making prayers their only duty.

The old man left for heavenly abode

leaving a void.

And memories of a decade

which shall never get decayed!

Poem-31

Lights that come during festivals

red, yellow, blue, green

colorful lights

look celestial

like the stars from the skies

that descended on Earth

sparkles up your life

especially when you

turn off your daily lights

they stand out better

Eventually pop, pop

they begin to fade

as the festivals go away

as you get back to your daily routine

cooking, cleaning, reading, drawing, knitting

back to your good old lights

the lights, yes, the lights

who may have felt left out

or just enjoyed the break

or who have accepted the ways of the world

Treating lights by their merit

by being attached

yet detached

to every light in your life

the ones that glitter

the ones that are boring

the ones that are temporary

the ones that are stubborn

the ones that are powerful

the ones that let you sleep through the night

But the ones you must

never, never ever

lose sight of

are the lights

that are the true lights

that glow from within

that guide you through every adversity

that permit you to seek every happiness

that Love you through your loneliness

that let you give every joy.

Poem-32

A child met happy one day

And the happy stuck

With a promise never to leave

The child smiled at

The dog, tree, flower, books, toys, friends,
bus, school

They all smiled back and stayed with him.

A child met anger one day

And the anger stuck

With a promise never to leave

The child shouted at

The dog, tree, flower, books, toys, friends,
bus, school

They all shouted back and ran away.

A child met sad one day

And the sad stuck

With a promise never to leave

The child showed a tear to

The dog, tree, flower, books, toys, friends,
bus, school

They all wiped the tear and went away.

A child met fear one day

And the fear stuck

With a promise never to leave

The child trembled at

The dog, tree, flower, books, toys, friends,
bus, school

They all trembled and fell apart.

A child met boredom one day

And the boredom stuck

With a promise never to leave

The child yawned at

The dog, tree, flower, books, toys, friends,
bus, school

They all yawned and fell asleep.

A child met lonely one day

And the loneliness stuck

With a promise never to leave

The child brooded to

The dog, tree, flower, books, toys, friends,
bus, school

They all sat in the corner and brooded away.

A child met confidence one day

And the confidence stuck

With a promise never to leave

The child showed the spring walk to

The dog, tree, flower, books, toys, friends,
bus, school

They all had a spring in their walk and
followed him.

Poem-33

Have you ever talked to the soil?

Have you ever buried a seed?

Have you ever watered the earth?

Have you ever collected water from nature?

Have you ever eaten food you grew?

Have you ever made a cloth from the cotton you grew?

Have you ever built a shelter?

If not

Time to upgrade your bucket list!

Poem-34

No payment made in kind or cash

For hard work and time spent

Just thank you from the bottom of my heart

For saving my life

by

Feeding a famished me

Lending hand to the fallen me

Sharing an umbrella to avoid wet me

No payment made in kind or cash

For hard work and time spent

Just sorry from the bottom of my heart

For not meeting your expectations

after

Giving desert to me

Advising already motorist me

Buying a downs jacket for cold me

Poem-35

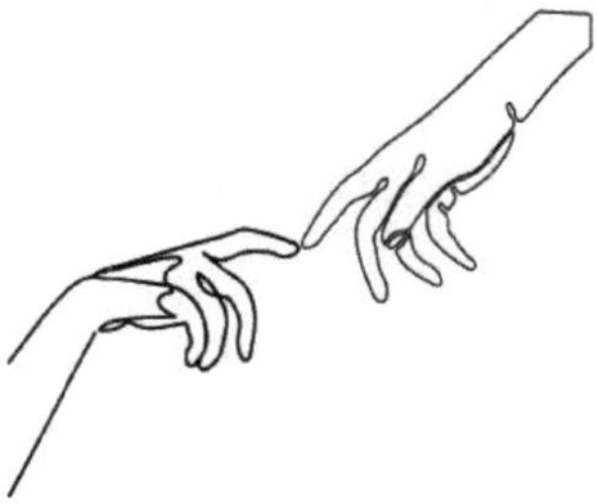

The last tip of her finger

Leaving her mother

Fear engulfing her eyes

She prayed for her mother

"I am not the only mother"

She ran with the rose

That stood alone at close

Until a girl her size picked it up

And her mother, she became!

The last grain of rice

Leaving her hand

Apprehensions engulfing her head

She prayed for her mother

"I am not the only mother"

She heard words like her mother

She ran for advice

That were ambiguous

Until hubby dear helped decode

And her mother, he became!

The last drop of knowledge

Leaving her mind

Anxiety engulfing her heart

She prayed for her mother

"I am not the only mother"

She smelt food like her mother

She ran for motivation

That got her confused

Until the kids in the class demanded

And her mother, they became!

Poem-36

Driving through Bandipur forest

Is the most pious rest

The body can invest

The lungs fall in love forever

The face that has never

Been kissed so gently ever

The ear hear

Decibels it was unaware

The fragrance no Christian Dior

Can bring to the nose so pure

The sight of every tree

That grew after exploration

Learnt to manoeuvre

Where need defines intake of water

Where animals hover

Who are not hoarders

Basic is the norm

Poem-37

The pain is killing

Suddenly my arms cradle a bundle of joy

Bringing a tear and a smile

Mama is going for bread and butter

Leaving bundle of joy with grandma

Bringing a tear and a smile

Bundle of joy is going to a play home

It is called "mother's touch"

Bringing a tear and a smile

Bundle of joy is going to a school

A drop in a big blue ocean

Bringing a tear and a smile

Bundle of joy is walking up to collect her
prize

After sacrificing her time to stand and stare

Bringing a tear and a smile

Bundle of joy set out for a six-day basketball tournament

Leaving her parents behind

Bringing a tear and a smile

"What is achievement?" I scream

A whisper says, "A cry and a laugh"

Bringing a tear and a smile

Poem-38

When a tiger attacks man

The tiger is shot down or caged

When a man attacks woman

The woman is killed or caged

I am proud to be a woman, anyway

Because I nurture life

By taking care of the weak

And being compassionate to them.

When a man wears modern clothes

He is learned

When a woman wears them

She is a “tradition breaker”

I am proud to be a woman, anyway

Because I nurture life

By accepting change

And being secure of them.

When a man goes out with a woman

Men are men and may go astray

When a woman goes out with a man

Blemishes are drawn on her

I am proud to be a woman, anyway

Because I nurture life

By respecting human beings

And being non-judgemental of them.

Poem-39

Walking through an avenue

Princess I was

Bridesmaids standing on either sides

Dressed in “Sharara”

Brown bottom and green top astound

Showering petals

The nearby trees were tall and fat

From where I stood

The distant trees were small and thin

Continuing the walk

The approaching tree got bigger

And turning around it's smaller

Walking through life's avenue

Princess I was

Situations standing on either sides

Dressed in "Sharara"

Brown bottom and green top astound

Showering resources

Views of afar-people were small

Judgemental emerges

Until near we come, glimpsing the big

Unprejudice emerges

Making the mind sound

Helping connection

Problems of nearby people are big

Sympathy flows

Until afar we go, grasping the small

Empathy flows

Making the mind sound

Bringing action

Let's walk and hold different position

Keeping eye on situation

We sure can deal with appreciation.

Poem-40

Once upon a time

Not so long ago

In a small town

Lived a colony of wild blue flowers

A sight that calmed the turmoil mind

Plenty of air

Purity of water

Vastness of green

With the right amount of blue

With no bondage

Children danced

Decorated their own hair

Created ikebana

The wild flowers enjoyed this game

Till the winter put them to sleep

Only to spring up next spring

To continue the wild games

A little frog croaked

About a lotus in a lotus pond

Seeking a friend

A wild blue flower seeking the same

Met with a pond

Full of pink lotuses on green pads

A sight so different

Different is enchanting

For an adventurer

The invitation from the lotus read:

"If my friendship is what you seek

Hop on to my green pad"

And in jumped the adventurer!

The intoxicating fragrance

Got her drunk

Swelling with pride

The minuscule greeted

All lotus lovers

Many a wind shook her pad

She felt breathless

The fragrance steadied her every time

One season of heavy rains

Flooded the pond

And the lotuses held on to each other

With many a push and pull

Looking to survive

The blue wild flower

Drenched and shaking

Crying for help

Haven't you adapted still?

How long would one take?

Adaption is key to survival

Look at us

We adorn Vishnu in the temples

And we don't cry

The wildflower gasping for breath

Looking for a berth

Until the lotus friend

Carried the blue wildflower to the banks

And placed her gently in the soil

She grows there alongside the lotus friend in the pond

And they lived happily ever after!

Poem-41

Relocating to a new place

Is exciting and filled with nervousness

Letting go and building familiarity

From amidst trees to no trees

Is disconcerting but transitional.

There is something about little things

That lifts one up

And in came the saplings

That filled the lonely and turmoiled mind

With embellishment

The little plants fluttered,

Shared and laughed with and at each other

Discussions ranged from Mother Earth to the sun

With big dreams ahead.

Days were filled with learnings

And nights were spent in slumber

Before we knew it

The saplings turned to trees

Of their own right,

They spread their arms

To declare their arrival

Eagerness to expand and accomplish

Wider and wider grew their arms

Until they scuffled and tugged.

The residents sought more sunlight

So pruning it was

And down came the branches

A big sigh of relief for the spared ones

Until the fall on a rainy stormy day

Pruning and falling is inevitable

Pruning is growing

Falling is letting go

Accepting each day as is

Feeling "mudita"

Meeting fear at the roots

The wisdom is indeed liberating!

Poem-42

I put my feet up and relaxed

without feeling guilty

I have achieved

and I have the right to bask in that glory

"What?"

asks many a questioning eyes

trained that they are

to see targets and results

to see money and bank balance

to see work and creations

But

I have learnt to

see and seek

contentment!

Poem-43

Tell me O wind

WERE

You so humble

Unaware of your power

And got carried away in your game

OR

Was it frustration of seeking recognition

That you so stormed through.

Tell me O tree

WERE

You so humble

To accept the floods

And transform your green-self to mere woody

OR

Was it the use of flood's fury

To set score with the monkeys.

Tell me O landslide

WERE

You so humble

To allow yourself the fall

And save the entire mountain from crumble

OR

Was it anger against mankind for the roads tunnels

That took to such destruction.

Tell me O death

WERE

You so humble

To stay away from the deathbed

To add many more moments to life

OR

Was it just stubbornness

That made life pay for shying away.

Poem-44

When I first set my eyes on her

I was insecure

She became less demanding

But not a word uttered!

Slowly and surely

This little sister of mine

Taught me that

Love multiplies when shared.

When I was growing up

I was the boss

She let me dictate

But not a word uttered!

Slowly and surely

This little sister of mine

Taught me that

There is joy in giving.

When she came out with my friends

I wanted my freedom

She followed in silence

But not a word uttered!

Slowly and surely

This little sister of mine

Taught me that

Life is also about accommodating.

When I was setting up my home

I wanted time to build

She gave me my space

But not a word uttered!

Slowly and surely

This little sister of mine

Taught me that

Love is unconditional!

When there was a crisis

I lost the ability to think

She handled with courage

But not a word uttered!

Slowly and surely

This little sister of mine

Taught me that

Faith can move mountains.

Poem-45

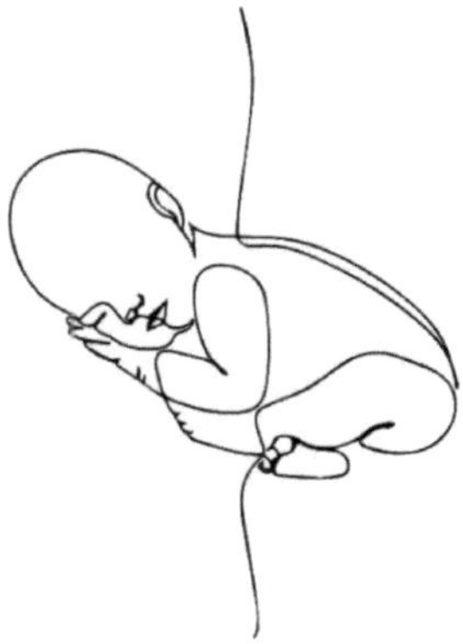

Infant I am

My head looking to survive

It yearns to learn movement

My heart looking to survive

It yearns for the love of an adult.

Toddler I am

My head looking to survive

It yearns to learn language

My heart looking to survive

It yearns for the love of grandparents.

Teenager I am

My head looking to survive

It yearns to have ambition

My heart looking to survive

It yearns for the love of a teenager.

Adult I am

My head looking to survive

It yearns to learn about money

My heart looking to survive

It yearns for the love of an infant.

Oldie I am

My head looking to survive

It yearns to have support

My heart looking to survive

It yearns for the love of a toddler.

Who am I today?

Infant, toddler, teenager, adult, oldie?

Poem-46

It is amazing that

From among a thousand faces you've met

Your mind stores this one face you met

Your eyes are in constant search for this one face.

It is amazing that

Not a handsome face, all agree

Your eyes don't seem to agree

Your eyes are in constant search for this one face.

It is amazing that

From among the hellos you made by handshakes

Your hand remembers only one handshake

Your eyes are in constant search for this one face.

It is amazing that

From a crowd making a fish market sound

Your ears pick up this one sound

Your eyes are in constant search for this one face.

It is amazing that

From even in stillness you are unaware of the heartbeat

Your body reacts to this one face by increased heartbeat

Your eyes are in constant search for this one face.

Poem-47

As seasons pass

I am standing in the garden

Filled with flowering plants.

Some of the flowers were young

Some were old

Some others growing together

Yet others to be born.

The mixed feelings were overwhelming!

And with all my efforts

I am standing in the garden

Living the different colors

Living the different fragrances

All of which are mine.

My happiness knew no bounds

Waiting for yet another season!

As seasons pass

I am standing in the garden

Filled with flowering plants.

Young flowers became old

Old ones withered away

Growing together flowers fell apart

None waiting to be born.

The mixed feelings were overbearing!

And despite my efforts

I was standing all alone in the garden

Reminiscing the different colors

Reminiscing the different fragrances

All of which were once mine.

My sadness knew no bounds

Waiting for yet another season!

Poem-48

One night

I went to sleep

In my dreams

I saw a huge tree.

The roots were made of

Oxygen, dust, water vapor

The trunk was made of

Mud, stones, water, coal, iron

The leaves were made of

Animals, insects, birds and man

Flowers were needs and wants

Fruits were inventions.

It looked so beautiful

I didn't want to wake up!

One night

I went to sleep

In my dreams

I saw a huge tree.

Leaves were working very hard

Generating flowers and fruits

Using the roots and trunks

Basking in their glories

Leaves were deaf to the cries

Parts of the roots were rotting

Barks on the trunk were holing

Some leaves were dying

The tree was tilting.

I woke up with a start

I didn't want to sleep again!

Poem-49

I am angry that

I am helpless at fifty

I am angry that

I learnt to manage anger

I learnt logic

I learnt to follow rules

I am angry that

I teach for money

I teach subjects to help children earn

I teach not, what money can't do

I teach not, celebrating self

I am angry that

Mankind continues to create

When there is plenty

Shifting basic needs

Flaunting riches

Making rules to protect wealth

I am sorry that

I am helpless at fifty

Poem-50

Teacher is a student

Student is a teacher

Desire to change

Willing to learn

Change is knowledge and comprehension

Change is application and analysis

Change is synthesis and evaluation

Change to think

Think to learn

Learn to identify

Happy, sad, fear, surprise, anger

Learn to accept

Learn to express

Learn to feel

Feel to change

Change is being aware and open-minded

Change is perseverance and connection

Change to experiment

Experiment to learn

Change to learn

Learn to change

Teacher is a student

Student is a teacher

Poem-51

Six in the morning

Trngggg goes the bell

In arrives my house help

No hi-hellos exchanged

Both of us are busy

Getting our lives moving

No conversations at all

With the exception of

Extreme emotional days.

And today is that day

One glance at her

Begins the flow of words

Her nephew is born

A very basic emotion indeed!

After an acknowledgement

I was only partially invested in her joy

But her joy was overflowing.

Until a sentence caught my attention

I hoped for a girl

My son could marry her

But my mother is very happy

Not having a girl child

The reason being my divorce

The trauma our family had

Will not be repeated

But that's sad

Just because I suffered

Doesn't mean everyone would

Life can also be beautiful

The biggest learning

Watching pain makes us weak

While suffering pain makes us tougher.

Watching pain makes us cynical

While suffering pain brings faith.

Watching pain makes us bitter

While suffering pain makes us see the sweetness of life.

As human beings we are here to do and not watch.

So the next time you have disturbing thoughts

It means we are watching and not doing.

Time to get started.

Do something worthwhile!!!!!!

Poem-52

Being rich

Is a state of mind

People with crores cannot sleep at night

While the homeless sleeps through the night.

People shoo stray dogs to dump food into the garbage

While the impoverished and the dog share the bread.

Poem-53

I am an angry person

I am a rude person

I am a reserved person

I am a selfish person

I am a lucky person

I am a generous person

I am a caring person

I am a capable person

I am a decisive person

I am a genuine person

Neither am I sweet

Nor am I a trash

Do not box me!

Poem-54

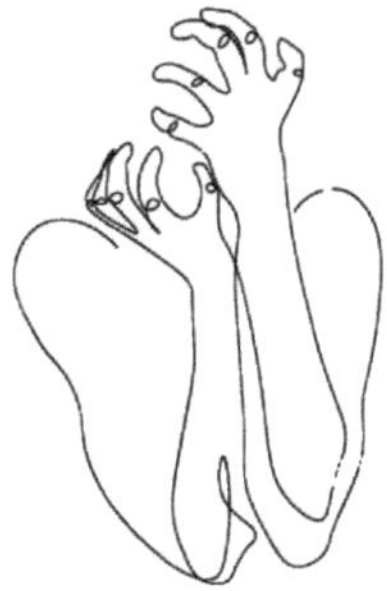

Being on the wrong side of right

Could still make you wrong

Being on the right side of wrong

Could still make you right

Being on the right side of right

Could still make you wrong

Being on the wrong side of wrong

Could still make you right

The paradox of life!

Poem-55

I want be a trash can

I want be a doormat

I want to be a fallen leaf

I want to be a torn dress

I want to be a rotten fruit

Let the ego go!

Poem-56

Standing alone

Can be scary

But is also a habit

Once you befriend

Yourself and faith

Once you learn to be

Secure and accepting

Life can be amazing!

Poem-57

In a room full of classical singers

A rock singer is minority

In a community of Diwali

Onam is minority

In a city full of people

Animals are minority

In a forest full of animals

Man is minority

In a region full of browns

Whites are minority

In a country full of citizens

Refugees are minority

Our experience of being

A majority or minority

Paves the way to make this world better

Treating others

The way we like to be treated

And not necessarily

The way we were treated.

Poem-58

The day my little girl was born

The love and responsibility

Of a different kind was born

At times love took over

At others responsibility took over

Thirty years after her birth

As she flew out of the nest

Memories of that love

Still brings smile on my lips.

The responsibility actions seem

Quite questionable!

Poem-59

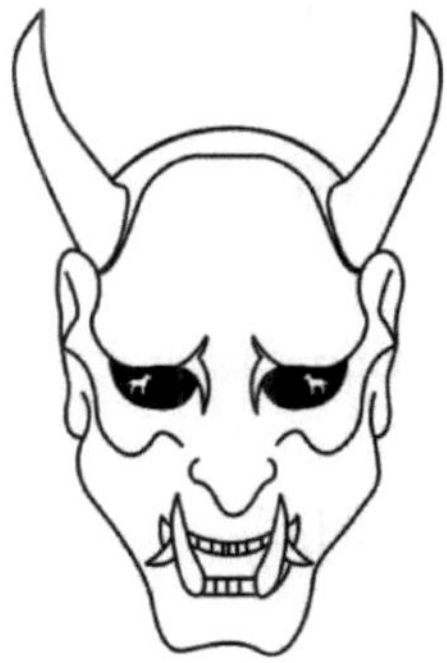

Protecting one's child

Is very instinctive

At times unnecessary stress

The minute the child walks

Mother's antennas are up

Hope there is no fall

Hope there are no sharp objects

Every time she misses

A sigh of relief

Protecting one's child

Soon becomes a habit

Looking out for dangers

Looking out for pitfalls

Seeing one's child

Dodging pretty well

Or getting up

After every fall

Dusting the back

Wiping the tears

And continuing the walk

A sigh of relief

Was it necessary protecting

A mother doesn't know

But what she learns eventually

Is building faith!

Poem-60

How are you?

Physically

Mentally

Because this could affect

What are you doing?

Physically

Mentally

Because this could affect

How are you?

A vicious cycle indeed!

Poem-61

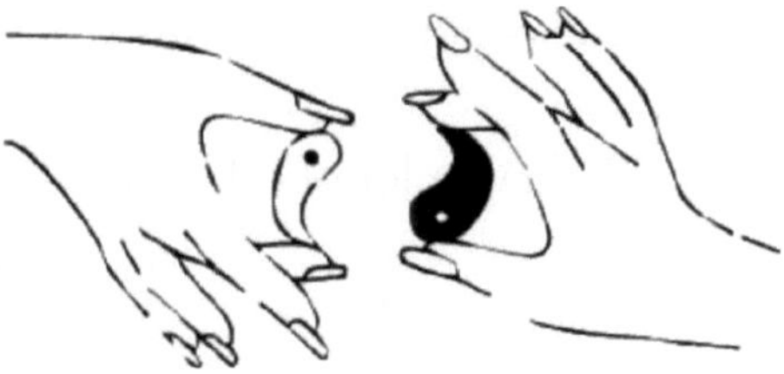

Sugar is an important ingredient in
everyone's life

It is an energy booster

Not too much

Not too little

Just the right amount

Keeps us going

I was a provider

You came to me

You paid for it

It was a transaction

Now I stopped keeping sugar in my store

Of course, I do have a lot of other things

But that's not your need

The transaction ended.

Poem-62

The company you keep matters

A room full of people

Could make you feel alone

All alone in a room

Could have you in good company.

Poem-63

Walking in the meadow

Looking at green

As far as eyes can reach

Seemed monotonous

Until the greens

Began walking towards me

Dark green leaves

Light green leaves

Apple green

Evergreen

Fern green

Honeydew melon green

Forest green

Praying mantis green

Moss green

Mint green

Pine tree green

Brewed tea leaves green

Many more greens

Waiting to be named.

Poem-64

I opened the door

Into a home I entered

There was nature

There was drama

There were people

I connected with

There were evils

I hated

There were times

I was on the edge

I was in la la land

There was eagerness

To reach to the end

To have a perfect ending

And with a smile

As I turned the

Final cover of the book

Something shifted

Inside of me.

I was happy to reach the end

And not so happy it ended.

Revisit I could

But the excitement of the first
Would not exist.

But I am sure

There will always be

Something new to discover.

If nothing else

I found another comfort home!

Poem-65

Knowing you have a bed to wake up in

Knowing you have food to eat

Knowing you have the mind to take on
challenges

Knowing there is water for your daily chores

Knowing you have people to talk to

Knowing you have oxygen to breathe

Knowing you have a bed to sleep at night

Is ultimate luxury

Anything beyond means

Time to give.

Poem-66

Seeing a double rainbow

They say is a sign of good luck

I second that

For the day I met my daughter

In flesh and blood

After a gap of two years

Double rainbows welcomed us

Or was it our meeting

That forced the rainbows to show up?

Poem-67

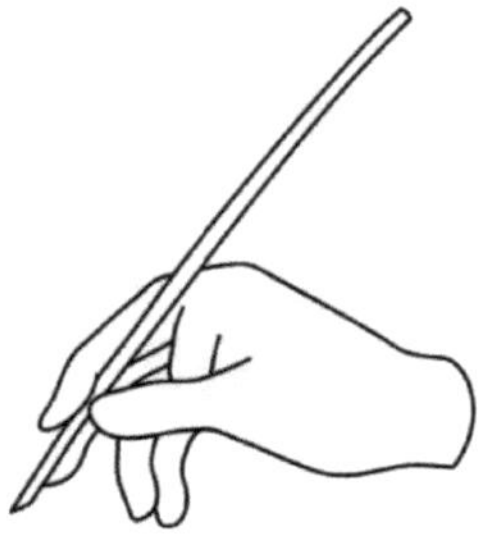

To all the sisters

Don't ever climb up the ladder

Stepping on a woman

Don't ever fall for a man

By pulling down a woman

Don't ever judge a woman in flesh trade

Without judging the men who go to her

Don't ever let others bring down a rising woman

With their frivolous talks

Don't ever let the world pass crude remarks

It is the body that procreates

Don't ever let anyone bully an angry woman

Anger is human emotion

Don't ever join the clan to rebuke her vice

Without rebuking vices in general.

Poem-68

Lie is bad

Lie is wrong

Do we do bad?

Do we do wrong?

How many lies do we say in a day?

I mean not the very big ones

The ones on the right side of the wrong

They are called white lies

How many times it has saved us

From embarrassments?

From spoiling our reputations?

From losing our friends?

Yet it doesn't get its due

The least we can do

To let it rest in peace is

Tell a sorry to lie!

9 789363 306233

Printed by Libri Plureos GmbH in Hamburg,
Germany